Aeroponics Gardening
for Beginners

Essential Guide On How To Grow Healthy Organic Fruits And Vegetables Without Soil

by
Kevin S. Stevenson

Kevin S. Stevenson
Aeroponics Gardening for Beginners

© Copyright 2022 by Kevin S. Stevenson - All rights reserved

This Book is provided with the sole purpose of providing relevant information on a specific topic for which every reasonable effort has been made to ensure that it is both accurate and reasonable. Nevertheless, by purchasing this Book, you consent to the fact that the author, as well as the publisher, are in no way experts on the topics contained herein, regardless of any claims as such that may be made within. As such, any suggestions or recommendations that are made within are done so purely for entertainment value. It is recommended that you always consult a professional prior to undertaking any of the advice or techniques discussed within.

This is a legally binding declaration that is considered both valid and fair by both the Committee of Publishers Association and the American Bar Association and should be considered as legally binding within the United States.

The reproduction, transmission, and duplication of any of the content found herein, including any specific or extended information, will be done as an illegal act regardless of the end form the information ultimately takes. This includes copied versions of the work, both physical, digital, and audio, unless express consent of the Publisher is provided beforehand. Any additional rights reserved.

Furthermore, the information that can be found within the pages described forthwith shall be considered both accurate and truthful when it comes to the recounting of facts. As such, any use, correct or incorrect, of the provided information will render the Publisher free of responsibility as to the actions taken outside of their direct purview. Regardless, there are zero scenarios where the original author or the Publisher can be deemed liable in any fashion for any damages or hardships that may result from any of the information discussed herein.

Additionally, the information in the following pages is intended only for informational purposes and should thus be thought of as universal. As befitting its nature, it is presented without assurance regarding its prolonged validity or interim quality. Trademarks that are mentioned are done without written consent and can in no way be considered an endorsement from the trademark holder.

Kevin S. Stevenson
Aeroponics Gardening for Beginners

Table of Contents

INTODUCTION 5

CHAPTER 1 - What is Aeroponics Growing? 7

CHAPTER 2 – How to Start an Aeroponic Growing? 13

    How to prepare the germination 16

    How to germinate seeds in rockwool cubes 18

CHAPTER 3 - Step-by-step Installation 21

    Lighting Installation 22

    Grow Room 27

CHAPTER 4 – Irrigation, Conductivity and Fertilization of the Aeroponic System 43

CHAPTER 5 - Hydroponics vs Aeroponics 49

CHAPTER 6 – Which Plants to Grow 57

    7 Ideas on Which Plants to Grow Indoors Directly at Home 58

CHAPTER 7 - Hydroponics Plantation 63

CONCLUSION 67

Kevin S. Stevenson
Aeroponics Gardening for Beginners

Kevin S. Stevenson
Aeroponics Gardening for Beginners

INTODUCTION

Congratulations on purchasing this book and thank you for doing so. This book is specially designed for those who want to build an aeroponic system and grow their own vegetables and ornamental plants at home in a simple and professional way. By creating an autonomous ecosystem.

Aeroponics is the method of growing crops above ground using nebulizers. The good thing is that the entire cultivation process is highly automated, but still requires very strict management.

The availability of lighting is also an important component in agricultural production. Adequate lighting is achieved by planting crops in vertical structures to maximize accessibility to light, while density and shading are kept to a minimum.

These growing conditions for plant cultivation, in terms of water, nutrients and light, are ideal for crops and maximise the usefulness of the growing area and use the space that might otherwise be unused. Having a mobile multi-level growing structure exposes the plants to ideal lighting during the growing season.

CHAPTER 1 - What is Aeroponics Growing?

Aeroponics is an indoor growing system, in a greenhouse or inside a grow box, where plants are grown without the use of soil, thanks to special systems characterized by a supporting structure, mesh pots in which plants are placed, nutritive solutions based on water and mineral fertilizers and air pumps. These are used to atomise the liquid solution, which - thanks to the action of the air - can reach the roots of the plants and nourish them in depth. Thanks to the aeroponic technique, it is possible to obtain ideal conditions for the development of plants. On the one hand, the closed and isolated environment will make cultivated plants much less susceptible to attacks from fungi and diseases, on the other hand, the roots will have a high level of oxygenation and can thus grow quickly with a minimum amount of water and mineral salts. Unlike in hydroponic cultivation, the plant is not irrigated - in the traditional sense of the term - with nutrients but suspended in a mesh pot from which the roots will come out, which will be periodically sprayed with nutrients. This system allows to consume even less water than what is usually used in a hydroponic cultivation system, because it is recovered and put back into the circuit thanks to a recovery system. Aeroponics is particularly suitable for all those crops that can develop vertically - thus avoiding contributing to soil exploitation - and less so for crops that need ample space, such as wheat and corn.

In an aeroponic system the plants develop outside the soil, they are continuously irrigated with the nebulization system, thanks to an immersion pump, in a completely controlled environment where the presence and spread of parasites and diseases, typical of soil cultivation, is very difficult.

Thanks to the constant and precise monitoring (with special instruments) of the fundamental environmental parameters (lighting, nutrition, temperature, humidity, pH and conductivity), it is possible to obtain significantly better results than normal cultivation in soil. All this without having to use - as in traditional crops - insecticides and pesticides that are potentially harmful to human and plant health (and with the relative consequences for the environment).

We would also like to remind you that the indoor cultivation technique using the aeroponic method allows to obtain extraordinary results in terms of speed and quantity, but also in quality.

But let's take a closer look, before referring you to the next chapters of this guide, at how - specifically - aeroponic cultivation works.

Kevin S. Stevenson
Aeroponics Gardening for Beginners

In this type of cultivation, the plants are placed in a system of PVC conduits - suitable for this type of cultivation - and installed at the top, supported by special panels, so that they remain suspended. At the base of these plastic conduit's nebulizers are placed, which will have the task of nebulizing the nutritive solution to the plants. The do-it-yourself aeroponic culture - which identifies a method but also a completely different way of growing, so much so that it is also called "aeroponic culture" - makes it possible to irrigate and feed the plants, making them grow healthy, without using chemicals and with a great saving of water. With all that this means for the health of our environment. It is no coincidence that the number of aeroponic cultivation in the world is constantly growing, so much so that there is an increase in aeroponic greenhouses.

In the water - which is sprayed with a special pump provided by the aeroponic system - all the essential nutrients to feed the cultivated plants are dissolved. The growth time of the plants is generally reduced compared to the growth and development time of plants grown in soil with traditional systems.

Kevin S. Stevenson
Aeroponics Gardening for Beginners

CHAPTER 2 – How to Start an Aeroponic Growing?

In order to be able to start cultivating with the aeroponic methods, it is necessary first to have all the necessary tools in the three phases of growth and development of the plant: the germination period, the growth period and, finally, the flowering phase.

Once you have studied all the phases and learned all the tricks to be able to grow indoors using the aeroponics method, you must have all the appropriate tools.

For the Germination Phase:

Necessary

- Mini greenhouse (to germinate seeds)
- Rockwool cubes (at least 1 per seed to germinate)

- Root stimulator

Optional

- Neon Light
- Watertight heating resistor (to keep the temperature of the mini- greenhouse stable at the optimum temperature of about 26 degrees).

For the Growth and Flowering Phase:

Necessary

- Indoor Lighting Kit (in chapter 4 we will explain how to choose the lighting system)
- Bulb/bulb
- Power supply
- Lamp/reflector holder
- Aeroponic system

- pH Meter/Test
- EC Meter/Test
- PH corrector
- Nutrients for the growth phase
- Nutrients for the flowering phase
- Timer for timing

Optional

- Thermometer/hygrometer
- Grow box / Grow Room or Mylar Cloth
- Get on and off (easy roller)
- Humidifier
- Fan

To set up the environment for the germination phase, the first and for some aspects the most important, it is necessary to get some rockwool cubes and the rootbooster, that is a product that - thanks to its composition - is able to stimulate and accelerate the development of the roots, strengthening them compared to a normal root system of a plant grown in soil.

How to prepare the germination

Combine 5 litres of water and 20 ml of a very powerful root development stimulator, which has the function of stimulating the growth of the root system.

With the liquid prepared, soak the rockwool cubes and leave them for about 24 hours to adjust their pH (which tends upwards, about 7.0).

The next day, remove the cubes from their solution and drain them well, so that the excess water comes out and oxygen enters, thus ensuring an adequate exchange of water and air.

push the seed to be grown into the hole inside the cube, to a depth of about half a centimetre.

Place the rockwool cubes in the mini- greenhouse you have purchased (or built according to the recommended criteria) and make sure that the temperature and humidity parameters are ideal for this phase: 26° with a high level of humidity (about 80%).

Place the neon lamp and keep it on all day (24 hours a day).

In the initial germination phase, the seed inserted in the stone wool cube does not need light, while it begins to need the action of the lamps when it starts to sprout and come out of the cube: it is essential to illuminate with a light that is not strong (preferably neon) or with special HPS and/or MH lamps, provided that the level of temperature and humidity is always checked.

If the plants do not receive adequate lighting, they will develop a much longer stem than normal. It can be said that the period needed to see the seed germinate is a minimum of two days and a maximum of two weeks. Remember not to touch the seed once it has been inserted and placed in the stone wool cube. Once the seed has developed, you will be able to see the roots that will cross the cube at the sides and bottom of the stone wool support.

If you want to use the propagation method for cuttings, we recommend this type of product: x-stream propagators of nutri cultures.

How to germinate seeds in rockwool cubes

Insert the seed into the hole (of the cube 4x4cm) at a depth of about 2cm.

At this point, it is necessary to cover and protect the cube inside a mini greenhouse or other container that can ensure that the temperature is kept around 26 and the humidity is high, about 80%.

The roots - once through the cube - will tend to come out from the sides and bottom of the cube. Depending on the use, the 4x4cm cube, once germinated, can also be inserted into the 7.5x7.5cm cube which has a 4x4cm hole on the top side (suitable for the smaller cube).

Once this first phase - i.e. the germination period - has been completed, the rockwool cubes can be used in any substrate (e.g. soil or coconut fibre) in hydroponic systems (clay, lapilli, perlite), or placed on NFT trays (i.e. a technique called Nutrient Film Technique that does not require the presence of the substrate).

The seed initially requires no light. Once the seedling comes out of the cube, however, it is essential to light it with gentle light (preferably with a neon light at a distance of about 1 cm) or an HPS and/or MH lamp (always monitoring both temperature and humidity).

Always remember that seedlings that do not receive adequate light tend to have a very long stem. Depending on the type, quality and age of the seeds, germination can take from 2 days to a maximum of 14 days. Always remember that the seed during germination is very delicate and should not be touched.

CHAPTER 3 - Step-by-step Installation

When the seed will have opened, thus ending the first phase of growth of the plant, it is essential to set up the aeroponic system in which to insert the cube of wool and the seed just germinated.

Today, on the market, there are many different aeroponic systems, but - in this specific case - we will take as reference and example the Amazon aeroponic system by Nutriculture, one of the most appreciated and sold, which is characterized by its advanced technology and the great results it is able to guarantee.

In any case, it is possible to use other systems; in this case it is advisable to follow the instructions provided by the manufacturer itself in the manual present in the product packaging.

How to set up the aeroponic system:

- fix the lower tank;
- put the pump inside the tank.
- place the upper tank;
- place over the perforated cover.
- connect the pump to the main connection and sprinklers.
- place the pots on the upper tank.
- connect the pump to the timer and to the mains.
- fill the tank with water and fertiliser (down a dedicated chapter).
- place the cube, with all the bud, in its pot.

Lighting Installation

At this point, it is necessary to illuminate the plant as soon as it comes out of the germination period: it is necessary to provide a lighting system to make the bud grow and bloom as if it were illuminated by natural sunlight.

A lighting system for aeroponic cultivation will consist of:

1. Power supply (or Ballast) to give an enough and pulse of current to turn the lamp on. Electronic ballasts - compared to ferromagnetic ones - have the advantage of:
   - consume less power.
   - heat a little.
   - be more stable and durable.
   - make wiring easier.
   - adjust the watts on some models.

2. Bulb (or bulb) to simulate the effect of the sun. There are various types of bulbs on the market for aeroponic cultivation. The

difference is in the technology used and in the different spectrum of light and colours. Remember that for vegetative growth you need a light spectrum tending to blue (MH lamps), while for flowering you need a light spectrum tending to orange/red (HPS lamps). Agriculture lamps are those that can be used in both growth and flowering phases (for this reason they are often recommended, because they are more comfortable and easier to manage).

3. Lamp holder and Reflector to support the bulb and diffuse the light - correctly and evenly - throughout the aeroponic growing area. Also, for this type of product there are various types on the market, but - in general - it is good to know that the two fundamental types of reflectors are air cooled and traditional ones (not air cooled).

Kevin S. Stevenson
Aeroponics Gardening for Beginners

In the table you can find a summary in order to find the right lighting system starting both from the cultivation space available (i.e. the size of the grow box or grow room) and from the number of plants grown inside it.

	150 Watt	250 Watt	400 Watt	600 Watt	1000 Watt
Plants number	1/2	2/4	3/6	4/10	8/18
m2	0.5	0.75	1	1.4	1.5
Grow room/ Box	70x70x180	80x80x180	100x100x200	120x120x200	240x120x200

Connect the power supply to the mains.

Electronic power supplies are simpler and more immediate to use, because they already have the connection to the electrical network ready, ferromagnetic ones are more complicated, because they must be wired manually.

Connect the ballast to the lamp/reflector holder.

The lamp holder to connect the ballast to the lamp is always equipped with a standard socket, called E40.

The lamp/reflector holder reflects and diffuses the light from the lamp. It is usually supplied with the entire lamp holder kit.

Screw the bulb to the lamp holder once wired, you must screw the bulb to the lamp holder and clean the bulb with a clean, dry cloth before turning it on.

Cultivation LED

The LED for cultivation can be used to grow any type of plant at any stage of development. The emission of white and red simulates the colour gradation on the orange tone, like an agriculture lamp.

The led has a higher cost than other products, but it has some advantages, such as current saving and the fact that it doesn't heat up; moreover, it is easy to mount and doesn't need power supplies and other supports.

Grow Room

A grow room is a growing area for indoor growing, even with the aeroponic system. You can grow indoors in any enclosed space, but you need to take several factors into account to ensure that all the parameters useful for the growth of the plant are regularly monitored and controlled to achieve the best possible result.

Here are the basic parameters to be monitored inside the grow box for indoor aeroponic growing:

- The light
- The temperature
- Humidity
- Ventilation, ventilation and carbon dioxide (CO_2)

The Light

The hours of light - and more generally the lighting in indoor aeroponic cultivation - is one of the most important factors because it is particularly decisive for the health and growth of plants.

Plants need the correct amount of light in order to simulate sunlight and feed the cultivated plants correctly.

The first step to take, in order to correctly manage and dose the hours and quantities of light, is to isolate the growing environment (for this reason it is recommended to use a grow box or set up a grow room correctly) in order to prevent the sun's rays from penetrating inside, a factor that will allow you to completely manage the artificial light and monitor it correctly. The presence of reflective mylar sheets inside the grow box or grow room will facilitate the uniform propagation of light within the growing area and will correctly illuminate the plants.

During the growing phase it is necessary to provide the plant with about 18 hours of light per day. In the third or fourth week of the growing phase it is possible to reduce the light hours from 18 to 12 hours: the plant will feel the arrival of autumn (thus simulating shorter light days) and will start flowering before winter arrives. In any case, it is not recommended to let the plant bloom when it is still too small and weak, as the structure and stem would not be able to support many flowers.

The timer is an indispensable tool for planning and activating the switching on and off lights within the indoor aeroponic growing area. There are many types of timers, from the most essential ones from a few euros to the more advanced ones, which cost of course a little more, but allow several additional features and definitely very useful. Among the cheap ones we find the analogy timers that allow you to plan within 24 hours but have limitations.

There are also digital timers that allow more detailed programming.

The Temperature

Among the basic parameters to be monitored within an indoor aeroponic cultivation area is the temperature (as in all indoor cultivation). The ideal temperature is between 21 and 28 degrees centigrade and you can monitor it with special precision instruments, such as thermometers or thermo hygrometers. Among the thermometers recommended to monitor the temperature of the grow box, there is definitely the digital one, with the minimum and maximum function, which allows you to check the temperature at any time of the day to verify the minimum and maximum temperature reached by the environment during the 24 hours. In this way it is possible to know the anomalies and run to the shelters.

But what should we do if the thermometer used indicates that the temperature is excessive? To lower the temperature inside a grow room it is possible to use a special vacuum cleaner or air extractor that sucks in the hot air in the room to push it outside, thus cooling the air in the grow room. The fan can be operated with a thermostat, so that it only works during the hottest hours, when the lamps are on.

If this doesn't lower the temperature either, you can think of an air conditioner.

What if the temperature is too low? To raise it, you can use an electric stove that can be adjusted and operated by a thermostat.

Humidity

Among the parameters to be constantly monitored there is of course - as mentioned above - also humidity, which is fundamental to ascertain the state of health and the correct development of plants grown indoors using aeroponic methods.

The humidity should be around 50-60%. To measure it correctly you should use a hygrometer, because if the humidity levels rise too high, you run the risk of mould, which causes damage to the plants.

If the humidity level should rise too high, it is advisable to use an air extractor (sucking in hot air also lowers the humidity). If the humidity level is too low, it is advisable to use a humidifier for the grow room.

Ventilation, ventilation and carbon dioxide

The movement, intake and extraction of air from an environment is one of the most important aspects of a hydroponic system and - more generally - in indoor plant cultivation, which is often not sufficiently taken into account when deciding to set up and start a new project.

Providing proper ventilation for your growing area is essential and vital for your greenhouse or environment, more commonly called a grow room. Adequate ventilation - and therefore proper air recirculation - inside the grow box is important for many reasons: temperature control, humidity, disease, odour control and air recirculation, which ensures a continuous exchange between the entry of fresh air and the exit of stale air.

Providing fresh air to the growing environment increases the amount of CO_2, which is essential for the survival and health of all plants. CO_2, in fact, represents about 50% of the dry weight of the plant, with oxygen accounting for the remaining 42%.

NOTE: Always remember that plants require CO_2 to grow healthily and - in the absence of this - the consequences are harmful.

You need to know that plants - within any hydroponics and indoor growing - will absorb the available carbon dioxide in a very short time, so it is essential to provide them with clean, fresh air to maintain adequate CO_2 levels and prevent them from dropping, which would greatly reduce the yield of the crop. Having small amounts of CO_2 results in slow growing crops and poor yields.

As well as increasing CO_2 levels, ensuring proper air circulation in your grow box - providing fresh air and allowing stale air to escape - reduces the risk of diseases developing in your greenhouse. It is good to remember that humid, stale air endangers the health of your plants.

It is no coincidence that diseases normally develop in environments where the air is still and humid, a situation that favours the development of dangerous diseases, dictated by the high level of humidity and the lack of air recirculation. If this aspect is not controlled and managed correctly, through a special ventilation for indoor environments, plants will tend to lose vigour and wither progressively.

In addition to what has already been seen, proper air recirculation inside the grow room or grow box - or greenhouse - is also essential to avoid the appearance and proliferation of insects, which normally cause serious damage to plants.

One way to minimize insect damage is to install a fan - fixed or rotating - dedicated to fresh air recirculation.

In essence, an efficient air recirculation system will provide plants with the correct level of carbon dioxide, allowing the development of strong, healthy roots that can absorb the necessary amounts of water and nutrients and - at the same time - minimize the damage caused by diseases and insects.

It should be remembered that the type and model of the ventilation system chosen for your hydroponic cultivation is a real priority in order to ensure abundant and quality harvests. The calculation that is made to identify the most suitable ventilation system for your growing area may be complex and require many variables. So, let's make it clearer and simpler by providing the key elements to identify the most suitable system. It should of course be borne in mind that, in general, the larger the cultivation environment, the more powerful the indoor ventilation system will have to be. Usually, two light grow rooms are used, but to know what kind of ventilation your plants need, it is essential to make some calculations.

Ventilation

The first thing to do - in order to find the right ventilation for your indoor cultivation - is to accurately measure the volume of your greenhouse - or your growing area - in cubic metres.

Once you have measured the length, width and height of your grow room, simply use the following formula to get the total cubic meters, the size of your room.

Length X Width X Height= Greenhouse volume in m2.

Let's make a practical example and assume that your greenhouse has the following dimensions: length: 3.65 meters, width 2.4 meters and height 2.5 meters.

multiplying these three values (3.65 X 2.4 X 2.5), the result will be 21.9 cubic metres.

On the other hand, it is good to remember that the more isolated the grow room, the better. A well-insulated environment will be easier to manage on an environmental level.

Below you will find a very simple tool to automatically calculate the flow rate of the ideal ventilation system for your greenhouse, depending on the parameters you need to enter.

The ventilation in the grow room and in general the recirculation of air is - as we have seen - a factor of primary importance. As written above - and in the other guides - good ventilation allows your grow air to avoid humidity accumulation and temperature rise.

The process of air extraction becomes, therefore, an indispensable element whose objective is the extraction of indoor air so that all the air is extracted every 4/6 minutes. An extraction system consists of the following elements:

- The extractor to extract the air from the grow box
- The extraction pipe or hose
- The fan for fresh air supply
- A fan (optional to improve air recirculation)
- An activated carbon filter (optional to eliminate odours at the outlet)

Aspirator

An air extractor must be chosen primarily according to the flow rate. To do the calculation, multiply the volume of the grow room (or grow box) by 75. To select the most suitable type of extractor you must multiply

Height x Width x Depth x 75 = Air extractor flow rate.

Once the flow rate has been calculated, you can select the recommended model for the growing space (grow box, grow room or greenhouse). You will then necessarily also need to buy the ducts - check the diameter - or choose the necessary reducers. To connect the extractor to the pipe/pipeline, use special connecting strips or resistant adhesive tape. Also, in this case, a timer should be used to adjust the control units and thus control the temperature and humidity levels.

Carbon dioxide (CO2) in the grow room

As mentioned above, when growing in a closed environment, there is a risk that the plants - when growing - consume a lot of carbon dioxide (CO2); if this happens, the growth of the plant will slow down considerably. In order to maintain high levels of Co2 it will be enough to let air from outside into the grow room with the help of an extractor. Often, however, excessive air recirculation causes the temperature to drop too low. In this case, it is possible to forcibly dispense carbon dioxide with the help of a CO2 cylinder dispenser.

Kevin S. Stevenson
Aeroponics Gardening for Beginners

CHAPTER 4 – Irrigation, Conductivity and Fertilization of the Aeroponic System

Irrigation is of course another extremely important aspect for the health and growth of plants in an aeroponic crop, because through irrigation - in addition to providing the necessary water - it also provides the necessary nutrients for the plant.

Therefore, it is essential to ensure water quality and control the two main parameters: pH and conductivity/Ec (electrical conductivity).

The pH must be between 5.8 - 6.0: with a pH meter you can see if the solution is acidic or basic.

If the solution is too acidic, it will have to be corrected with pH+, if the water is too basic, it will have to be corrected with pH-.

pH- with 30% phosphoric acid to lower the pH value of the nutrient solution.

pH + with Potassium carbonate to increase the pH value in the growth and flowering phase.

The electrical conductivity (EC) is measured in mS/sec milli-Siemens per second with a special instrument, the conductivity meter. The measurement of this value is essential because it identifies the amount of salts dissolved in the water.

The salts naturally present in tap water generally vary from zone to zone, so it is recommended to use osmotic water or water filtered with a special reverse osmosis system. In this way the water values bring the electrical conductivity close to zero.

The recommended conductivity values change between germination and growth/flowering phases.

In the germination phase the Ec should be between 0.6 and 1.0.

In the growth and flowering phases between 1.0 and 2.0.

In the last flowering phase, it is advisable to go down as in the first phase, between 0.6 and 1.0.

When the electrical conductivity is too low you need to increase the amount of fertilizer, if it is too high you need to decrease the fertilizer.

Water temperature is another important factor in hydroponic and aeroponic cultivation: it should be between 15 and 23 degrees centigrade.

Fertilisers and nutrients are crucial for plants in indoor growing because - unlike plants in soil - those grown on substrates other than soil need to take their nutrients elsewhere.

There are so many types on the market, the important thing is to make sure that the ones we want to use are designed - and therefore suitable - for plants grown in aeroponics and hydroponics.

Below are the doses and how to use the fertilizers to be used during the growth and flowering phases.

In the diagram Cellmax products are used (in case you decide to use another brand it is advisable to follow the instructions on the package): in the summary below are indicated the various weeks, the products and the doses to be administered.

- CellMax Rootbooster 0.5L
- CellMax HYDRO Grow 2x1L
- CellMax HYDRO Bloom 2x1L
- Cellmax Superenzyme 0.5L
- Cellmax P-K Booster 1L

Kevin S. Stevenson
Aeroponics Gardening for Beginners

CHAPTER 5 - Hydroponics vs Aeroponics

Hydroponics and aeroponics are both extremely efficient techniques for the cultivation of plants without the use of soil and, therefore, allow to cultivate everywhere, even where there is no soil.

They can be applied both indoors (indoor growing) and outdoors (if the right climatic conditions are in place) and all that is needed to grow the plants is to develop a nutrient solution based on water and nutrients. Even better if the irrigation and feeding process of the plants is managed through an automatic system, so that the continuous intervention of a person in charge is required.

Hydroponics: specific characteristics

In hydroponic cultivation - as already discussed in our guides, manuals and blog articles - plants are grown without soil and with the use of water. Actually, it is good to know that there are different types of hydroponic systems, which use different structures and elements, but - in general - it is possible to say that with this technique plants grow thanks to the action of water enriched with nutrients. In a first period, the plants are started inside inert substrates, such as coconut fibre, perlite, expanded clay, or other materials useful for the realization of substrates, and then pass inside hydroponic systems, which provide - in addition to water supply - also a proper lighting, thanks to the presence of ad hoc lamps, temperature, humidity and proper ventilation of the environment.

Aeroponics: specific characteristics

Aeroponics is an alternative form of cultivation of plants, vegetables and fruits that does not require the use of soil or water.

With this cultivation technique, in fact, plants live and grow brilliantly and healthily thanks to the nebulization of a nutritive solution, based on water and substances useful for growth, which are delivered to the roots with a special sprayer. This technique should not be confused with hydroponics, where the most important element is not air - as in this case - but water.

Once the aeroponic system is set up, the plants are suspended with the roots in the air inside a grow room (or cultivation chamber) where they will remain until harvesting time.

Underlying the growth and health of the plants is certainly the constant control of temperature, humidity and lighting.

Pros and Cons of Hydroponics

The advantages of using a hydroponic system are certainly the reduced maintenance, the possibility to grow at any time of the year and the opportunity to control the climate of the growing environment.

More generally, the great advantage of hydroponics is in complete control over nutrients and, therefore, plant growth. In addition, hydroponically grown plants have a better yield than plants grown in soil. Many such systems recycle water and reduce waste.

In fact, these soil-free growing systems use only 10% of the amount of water needed for conventional crops and are easy to build and assemble. Hydroponic gardens do not require the use of herbicides or pesticides, precisely because no weeds grow there, they need little space and are not dependent on the growing seasons, because they use lamp light, which can be installed anywhere.

However, hydroponic gardens have drawbacks; for example, if the temperature is too high or too low, even for just one day, plants could die or suffer serious damage. In addition, the purchase of hydroponic systems and accessories may be expensive, especially if you are not an expert.

Pros and Cons of Aeroponics

Among the advantages of aeroponics is - in absolute first place - the efficiency and cleanliness of the growing environment.

With this technique, in fact, you get excellent and flourishing harvests in a short period of time. Another important advantage is the very low risk of contracting diseases and bacterial infections. On the other hand, a disadvantage - especially if you are a beginner - lies in the rather high cost, because it requires the purchase of a series of equipment. In addition, you need a dedicated indoor room in which you can install the aeroponic system.

Hydroponics and Aeroponics: Similarities and Differences

Hydroponics and aeroponics have a lot in common: aeroponics are - in fact - a hydroponics culture, which also uses the benefits of air. To simplify and summarize, we can say that aeroponics is an evolution of hydroponics, to get the most out of the potential of plants in terms of yield and speed.

The main difference between the two techniques is that hydroponic systems come in many forms: plants can be suspended in water full-time, or they can be fed by a continuous or intermittent flow. In a hydroponic system, plants grow with water and without soil, with the help of inert substrates. The two systems have in common the supply of nutrients that are delivered directly from the source and supplied to the roots.

Plants in aeroponics, on the other hand, are never put into water, but are sprayed remotely thanks to a dispenser that hydrates and nourishes the roots several times an hour, thanks to an automated system that guarantees their regularity and punctuality. One reason why these two cultivation methods have so much in common is that aeroponics is a type of hydroponic cultivation. The main difference is that hydroponic systems can be of various types: there are different types and for this reason you can choose the one that best suits your needs.

A common disadvantage of both hydroponic and aeroponic growing systems is that - relying on automated systems that require electricity - they may require the use of expensive generators, which can be used in the event of power outages. However, once set up and started up, hydroponics and aeroponic systems can make significant savings compared to traditional growing techniques.

According to current phenomena, it is possible that forms of hydroponic and aeroponic agriculture will increase in popularity over time and become commonplace in the homes of all of us. It is certain that - due to climate change and the unregulated action of man - the amount of soil available for cultivation will tend to decrease and its quality will continue to deteriorate, so more and more people will try to produce healthy food in their homes (many have already started growing salads, tomatoes, strawberries, etc.). Hydroponic and aeroponic gardens and gardens can provide the right answer to these growing needs.

CHAPTER 6 – Which Plants to Grow

Aeroponic cultivation is becoming increasingly popular. Due to its ability to adapt to many different situations such as the absence of green space or unfavourable weather, more and more space is being made available for cultivation, becoming the preferred solution for many.

The ecosystem that is created inside a grow box can offer the plant everything it needs to be able to grow luxuriant and healthy. All plants grown indoors, in fact, are grown without the use of pesticides. A great benefit that eliminates the risk of water, air and soil pollution.

Not all plants, however, are easy to grow at home: succulent plants, for example, need a drier soil as do some bulb plants. So, let's see which plants are

7 Ideas on Which Plants to Grow Indoors Directly at Home

Light Cannabis

The most cultivated plant in indoor aeroponics is certainly the legal hemp: with this cultivation system it will be possible to obtain even 4 or 5 harvests per year, optimizing the production to the maximum.

To start the cultivation of hemp, it is essential to choose only and only seeds certified at European level. Growing it indoors always allows you to produce it non-stop and have a controlled product in every aspect and always of the same high quality.

To learn more about how to grow medical cannabis legally.

Microgreens

Considered by many to be the food of the future, microgreens or micro-gifts are very young small plants of different types of vegetables that are perfect for indoor aeroponic cultivation. They are harvested at a more advanced stage of ripeness than sprouts.

It is possible to grow them without the need for specific agricultural knowledge, they are suitable for all seasons and with the help of LED lamps they grow strong and fresh. Ideally, they should be harvested after a period of 7 to 20 days after sowing. Rich in vitamins and minerals, they are perfect in the kitchen, so much so that even great chefs often use them.

Peppers

Another perfect vegetable for aeroponic cultivation is pepper. With all its bright colours, this vegetable can be grown at home for a steady harvest and full of vitamin C and antioxidant properties.

With the use of a grow room, in fact, you can recreate the ideal environment for these plants to grow strong and tasty. With the use of LED lamps, you will be able to have pepper on your table all year round, not only in summer as it normally happens, and with all its organoleptic characteristics intact.

Tomatoes

The most common product in aeroponic cultivation after hemp is certainly the tomato, a great protagonist of the Mediterranean diet. With this type of cultivation, you don't have to wait for the right season, but you can enjoy the fresh taste of the tomato whenever you want, to put in salad or to make preserves.

According to recent studies, moreover, tomatoes grown indoors with the help of LED lights seem to grow richer in nutrients than normal vegetables grown in the garden or vegetable garden. Compared to sunlight alone, LED bulbs, if properly adjusted, can reach certain points on the plant otherwise hidden, thus exploiting all the potential it offers.

Decorative plants

Ornamental plants embellish the house and in an aeroponic cultivation they can grow more and more beautiful and dense. In this case green leafy plants such as Ficus or pothos are ideal. They are easy to grow indoors and very ornamental.

Aromatic plants

Another idea for aeroponic cultivation is to choose aromatic plants, which will fill the nostrils and dishes of your kitchen with their good smell. Basil, rosemary, parsley: choose the herbs you prefer and start your cultivation. It will be enough to keep under control especially temperature and humidity to always have with you your favorite aromas.

Orchids

Finally, the delicacy of orchids finds a perfect environment in aeroponic cultivation. Even those who have fewer green thumbs will be able to grow this beautiful flower at home in all its different species. Among these, epiphytic and terrestrial orchids are particularly suitable.

Growing them at home is an excellent solution, which allows you to stem some problems that might otherwise occur in the presence of soil and increase the quality of the plant itself.

CHAPTER 7 - Hydroponics Plantation

The term Hydroponics was re-invented in the mid-twentieth century. The concept of plants growing without soil dates back to prehistoric times. The mythical hanging gardens of Babylon, the floods of the Nile and the floating gardens of Mexico City are all examples of hydroponic systems. History, as always, has transformed the circle and the age of hydroponics has returned to our times.

Why use this type of cultivation?

1. Nutrition - abundant, no deficiencies or toxicity. You can have total control over the administration of hydroponic fertilizers.
2. Yield - 2 to 10 times more than growing in soil! Super speed in growth with an abundant final yield.
3. Water - saving 80%. You don't have to water every day; it is the same water that is used and recirculated by an irrigation system.
4. Diseases - no soil viruses or bacteria. In the absence of soil and organic matter there are almost no diseases.

5. Weeds - practically none. Inability of weeds to grow in the hydroponic system.
6. Quality - higher, better, healthier. Thanks to the absolute control of the values the plant grows in the best way increasing the quality and the final taste.
7. Maturity - you can choose, it is not seasonal, faster! Possibility to grow in continuous cycles 12 months out of 12.

How hydroponic cultivation works

The plants are grown in a sterile inert growth medium, such as rockwool, clay, perlite, vermiculite and fed with a mixture of water and nutrients. The principle is fundamental, plants that are grown in soils must continuously develop their root system in search of water and nutrients so most of the plant's energy is used for root development and limits its superior growth. Consider that water, nutrients and air is supplied directly to the plant, freeing it from unnecessary energy expenditure and giving it a balance between root and stem. By giving all the nutrients, air and water you could want, your plants grow much faster and with an optimal yield equivalent to 100%.

Kevin S. Stevenson
Aeroponics Gardening for Beginners

The key to your success for optimal hydroponic growing is light, air and nutrient solution. The nutrient solution is, in other words, water with nutrients. It must contain all the mineral elements necessary for plant growth and must be in the right proportions. Nothing can be left to chance. Fortunately, there is a wide range of hydroponic fertilizers available and it is simply a matter of choosing the product that best suits your needs.

Useful tips for success in hydroponics

For a good start, it is imperative that quality water is inserted into the system tank. The tap water must be checked with an EC and TDS meter. If the value exceeds 150ppm a reverse osmosis filter should be used.

In addition, the amount of oxygen in the water is very important for plants and we recommend using an oxygen pump.

Another tip is to give the plants, in addition to the classic N-P-K fertilizers, boosters rich in vitamins and microelements that can enrich the life cycle of the plants themselves. For the flowering phase, in addition to the classic fertilisers, you can also use a booster that can double the flowers or fruits of your plants, the BioBizz Top Max.

Remember that the pH and ec of the solution should be measured daily and the solution should be replaced once every 2 weeks. Also remember that the pH of the solution tends to increase with nutrient administration, so it is recommended to measure the pH after adding fertilizer to the solution.

Usually before harvesting hydroponics growers tend to purify the plants. This can be done by replacing the nutrient solution with simple water for the last 7 /10 days. This technique called "flashing" allows you to remove any fertilizer in the plant tissue and improves the taste and aroma of the final product.

CONCLUSION

Thank you for coming all the way to the end of this book, we hope it has been informative and able to provide you with all the tools you need to achieve your goals, whatever they may be.

Aeroponics has emerged as a great way to achieve the growing of genuine and tasty plant products at home for good health. Yet, many people fail to get all the benefits of this wonderful process due to lack of knowledge of the process. This book has tried to bring all the important points to the fore so that you can get all the benefits of aeroponics without having to deal with the negative effects.

All you must do is follow the information provided in the book and follow the directions.

You can also get all the benefits of the process by following the simple steps in the book.

I hope this book will really help you achieve your goals.

Kevin S. Stevenson
Aeroponics Gardening for Beginners

Kevin S. Stevenson
Aeroponics Gardening for Beginners

Kevin S. Stevenson
Aeroponics Gardening for Beginners

www.ingramcontent.com/pod-product-compliance
Lightning Source LLC
Chambersburg PA
CBHW070336120526
44590CB00017B/2906